PARADISE MOMENTS

Edited by

Heather Killingray

First published in Great Britain in 2002 by
POETRY NOW
Remus House,
Coltsfoot Drive,
Peterborough, PE2 9JX
Telephone (01733) 898101
Fax (01733) 313524

Copyright Contributors 2002

HB ISBN 0 75432 776 0
SB ISBN 0 75432 777 9

FOREWORD

Although we are a nation of poets we are accused of not reading poetry, or buying poetry books. After many years of listening to the incessant gripes of poetry publishers, I can only assume that the books they publish, in general, are books that most people do not want to read.

Poetry should not be obscure, introverted, and as cryptic as a crossword puzzle: it is the poet's duty to reach out and embrace the world.

The world owes the poet nothing and we should not be expected to dig and delve into a rambling discourse searching for some inner meaning.

The reason we write poetry (and almost all of us do) is because we want to communicate: an ideal; an idea; or a specific feeling. Poetry is as essential in communication, as a letter; a radio; a telephone, and the main criterion for selecting the poems in this anthology is very simple: they communicate.

CONTENTS

ONE WISH

Greater than
The greater self
Composite companion
To itself.
Wealth greater
In Harmony
Set above for
All to see.

Nicola Barnes

I'D GIVE . . .

I'd give my world
Just to be happy
I long to smile
To feel sunshine radiate deep inside.

I'd give my world
Just to feel alive
To have something beautiful growing inside.

I'd give my world
To be a contented fool
Yet I'm too aware
In my world of dreams
I long to be happy
I'd trade my life
To feel a moment's happiness.

Shakti Kissoon

FOREVER FRIENDS
(Dedicated to my grand-daughter)

So now you've made it to twenty-one
Your life has been a mixture of sadness and fun
You've bought a car - well maybe a few!
You've got a flat - well a room with a view!
You have found many friends and you'll find lots more
As you travel your life and open new doors.
Friends make life a lovelier place to help you get
Over each problem you face
They are there when you need them to brighten your day
To always believe in you - come what may.
When life's not so rosy they'll give you a hand
They will cheer you and help you - whatever you've planned.
When you're feeling down they'll be there with a smile - helping you
Realise that life is worthwhile.
Time will bring changes to your life - you'll meet a man,
become his wife.
You may become a mother with children to look after
To cuddle and care for and share hours of laughter.
Your life will be full with love beyond measure
With a husband and family to always treasure
But remember that life you had before -
Don't push it away and close the door.
The happiness you shared will never end
Remember them always
Your Forever Friends.

Elsie Francis

FOR YOU ARE MY FRIEND

I miss you when you go away
For you are my friend
You are always there in my time of need
For you are my friend.

You are honest, loyal, a friend so true,
For you are my friend.

What can I give to you?
How can I repay it all?
By being your friend too!

Victoria Sisam

LINDA COMING HOME

The haunting drone of the plane
We raced to Gatwick
Only to find
Time had taken the hours away
That should have been ours
Never to recapture the
Breathless moment of a step
Not heard in months,
Memories we shared, we
Found later, stronger and
More poignant for waiting.

Joan Hands

MIKE - THIS IS FOR YOU

I've never had a friendship,
As close to me as you,
You've opened up the blinds,
And let the light shine through.

You've reached inside my soul,
Searched for what is there,
You've removed the bricks around me,
And shown you really care.

We do not need to speak,
An understanding and a peace,
We have in silence,
And yet again in speech.

I value what we have,
The way you make me feel,
I hope that it's the truth,
The way we are so real.

Something links us,
A bond between us,
We are tied together,
Unconditionally forever.

I'll always be there for you,
Whatever day or night,
Whatever the reason,
To laugh or to cry.

I miss you when you're far away,
I treasure the moments when we're near,
A friendship that I hope will never die,
Not this nor any other year.

Hannah Freeman

FRIENDSHIP

Friendship is amazing,
It lights your darkest day
When we can't see,
The wood for trees,
Friendship will guide the way
Although we see things differently
We really see the same
Just sit back upon your chair
Look through a mirrored frame
From you I ask for nothing
But everything I give
You helped me through
My trauma times
You showed me how to live
So happy birthday Noreen
From the bottom of my heart
I hope our friendship
Stays this way
And now we'll never part.

M J Morgan

TONI

You are a close friend to me
Even though I don't know you that well
I can talk to you about anything
You help me escape this hell.

You're really funny
And really sweet
You're so sarcastic,
You're really neat.

You make me laugh
Until it hurts
I can't believe that
I didn't like you at first.

I'm so glad we're friends
You are special to me
Even though you don't believe it
It's great you like me for me.

I can be myself around you
And you don't mind one bit
You think I don't like you
But I'm so glad you're my friend.

Jodie McKane

THE TWO OF US FOREVER!

Whenever I'm with you, my heart skips a beat!
You're the one who makes me feel complete.
In times of sorrow, I turn to you,
You calm me down, you disperse my blues!

You are my strength, my love, my whole life!
My one and only, darling wife!
Who else could care so much for me?
I feel so proud, so alive, so free!

Throughout life's journey, right till the end,
Stay with me, my dearest friend!
Together, there's nothing we can't do,
The world's out there, for just us two!

Whatever fate throws, we will take it,
Two of us together, we're sure to make it!
So much in love, and always together,
Joined by the heart, today and forever.

R Ninnis

TO A FRIEND

To me you are my dearest friend,
And I hope our friendship will not end.
You know me better than most,
Of a better friend I can't boast.
Even when we argue or even fight,
I know you will be there some lonely night.
It may take hours or even days,
No matter what other people say.
You give me the most love I've ever had,
When we disagree I feel really bad.
You know what I really think of you,
And I hope you feel the same way too.
You stuck by me through some hard times,
And even when I've committed crimes.
You listen to me when I want to talk,
And walk with me when I want to walk.
I know you treat me like a brother,
And to me that's better than my mother.

Robert J Melvin

SORROW

My husband's just died
And I'm feeling quite ill
There's a hole in my life
That nothing can fill.
A friend and a lover
Both rolled into one
How can I continue
In this life all alone?

We were young when we met
Fifty years we spent together
We had our little tiffs of course
But we braved the stormy weather.
I know he's watching over me
And helps me keep on track
The thing I cannot understand
Is why he's never coming back?

A loving family was all we craved
A happy and peaceful life
We never wanted anything special
We were happy as man and wife.
The memories I have are all special
Nothing will make them grow dim
There's only one thing that I want now
That's to live up in heaven with him.

I Kenny

FRIENDS

They come in various sizes and shapes
With a sprinkling through every age
Everyone's a 'friend' when we're so young
Saying 'my friend' was all the rage.
From 'tots' to 'teens' one is always 'in love'
A relationship starts and then dies
A constant upheaval of teenage friends
And all those tragic goodbyes!
Then life settles down and true friends emerge
With qualities no one can doubt
And one always knows that in times of stress
They'll immediately seek you out
With help and solace - whatever one needs
Or perhaps a mere listening ear
And maybe a shoulder that's strong and broad
Some words to help banish each fear.
Families too can be friends - just like mine
Who are always on hand when I call
But won't intrude when I want to be free
Yet they are there - whate'er may befall.

Elsie Sharman

BELIEVE

You mean so much to me my friend,
your kisses warm and sweet,
I love your smile, your special ways,
you'll always be complete.

The things you say, the things you do,
I can't believe it's real,
you'll never know how much you mean
or how you make me feel.

If ever we should drift apart,
I hope we never do,
I'll go on loving you my friend,
forever through and through.

Babs West

SPECIAL FRIEND

My special friend, my heart is aching,
To know deep inside, your heart is breaking,
We've talked and talked, and cried so much,
But deep inside you is the pain I cannot touch.

You pour out your fears to my receptive ears,
As you don't know how to face the coming years.
You go through the motions of life's treadmill,
But underneath the time stands still.

Yet, you forget, I've been there too,
The times, when I did not know what to do,
I was lost, so many years ahead,
And life without him, was something to dread.

The pain's still there, without love, it could not be,
But love is stronger then death, just wait and see.
Touch her face in your dreams, and
She will be there, to watch over you, believe me.

Anne Roberts

THE JOY OF FRIENDS

A true and loving friend
Is a joy that lasts a lifetime
A feeling that does not end.

Happy hours spent together
Enjoying all life's gifts
I hope it lasts forever.

Till time does not exist
Thank you Lord for all our pleasures
Life was all that we had wished.

June Clare

TOO LATE TO TELL YOU

When I was young you told me words to show the way, now I know I
should have listened to what you say.
Every day I pray for tomorrow for you to show me the way
and ease the sorrow.
Although life goes on, I feel empty now you're gone.
Words that haven't been shared, they were said too late;
Now all I can do is leave it to fate!
I tried to make up to you in a way I could, but I never said,
'I love you,' like I should.
As long as I can remember, we've always been together,
I can't say goodbye, it's hard to know how.
I cry each day for you and hope there's no pain,
all is different, and nothing feels the same.
A scent in the air makes me know you're near,
and I still see your face and that roaming tear.
You have known for a while, you'll soon be gone
and yet you kept fighting strong.
The pain will never go from the emptiness inside,
Nothing will be the same Granny since you died.
Every day I think of you remembering all you do,
the unknown sound I often hear reminds me of you
and I have no fear.
A part of me is gone, yet the love for you keeps growing strong.

Kelly Stephens

FRIENDS

Friends are the ones who are special,
Their nearness makes you feel tall.
They're always there when you need them,
And never grumble at all.
They pick you up, when you're flagging,
And bring you back into line.
They do it without any nagging,
And can make a rainy day shine.
You don't have to ask for a favour,
It's given without any plea.
Their steadfastness, you can just savour,
A trade that comes without fee.
Treasure these gems of acquaintance,
Their priceless, so treat them with care.
And you will have the assurance,
Of knowing they'll always be there.

Duchess Newman

A FRIEND FOR LIFE

Together we struggled with the intricacies of algebra,
In geography we studied the globe from pole to pole,
In history kings and queens tumbled about in our heads,
Gaining Higher School Certificates was our goal.

Sixty years ago we were grammar school friends,
Laughing at successes, the failures we bemoaned,
It was wartime, the future uncertain,
We lived for the day, tomorrow was unknown.

Triumphant, prized certificates in hand, we parted,
Many miles and milestones to come between,
News of husbands and children welcomed in Christmas letters,
Thoughts and wishes sent to a friend unseen.

Great excitement with a proposed recent visit,
Now grandmas, me with two grandsons, her with more.
We'd catch up where we left off in the forties,
Who was this frail, old woman opening the door?

Where was the bubbling energy and curls of yesterday,
The exuberance and chatter which knew no end?
Now a familiar glint in the eye, a massive bear hug,
Years vanished, here was the same dear friend!

Pat Heppel

WHAT IS A FRIEND?

A friend is someone who you can share your innermost fears with
Someone who can give you confidence when you feel doubt
Someone who can tell you when you are wrong
Without making you feel small.

When you are sick and feel alone
A friend will welcome you into their home
Someone you can fight with and forgive you without holding spite
Someone who is there for you when everyone else is against you.

If you yourself be honest in word and deed
A friend can believe in you
This is truly what a friend means to me
If by chance you should meet someone like that
Then you have gained a friend.

Sylvia Brown

A FRIEND INDEED

Ah yes. So is that one way to go?
You apply like this. There now
And then after, to a different address
When you've finished there
After many hours and many days.
You're quite well up, in spite of your age.
You know all about computers and software packages.
I may still be young but you are ahead in years as well.
A family friend, you've wisely told
What to look at, to try, to use.
You talk of the centre that gives job training
And are a friend indeed in this and other questions
Still remaining.

C J Bayless

FRIENDSHIP

There are many jewels in this world,
Many treasures without end,
But all these things cannot compare
With the joy of having a friend.

No matter what you do in life,
Or how many miles you wend,
Your greatest satisfaction lies
In the joy of being a friend.

You've been through life together,
Met and helped wherever you can,
That's been the way, in all the years
Since the friendship first began.

Isobel E Crumley

TO A GUIDE DOG

They tell me your coat is golden,
Bright as a summer's morn;
I feel the light and warmth from you
Just as I sense the dawn.

Your eyes are brown, so people say
Reflecting love and trust.
I know you'll always lead the way,
To follow you - I must.

I feel your tail against my skirt,
You're pleased that I'm aware.
I bend and stroke the worthy back
And tell you that I care.

Your cold, wet nose is ever near,
It searches for my hand;
I stroke the noble head I hold
- It's love you understand.

You lick my hand to say you're there
- Your presence reassures me;
Those eyes are mine beneath my touch
- Those eyes are mine - you see.

Not sight, but touch must be our way
As one through life we blend;
Together, now and every day
- Firm friends until the end.

Mary Farrell

MY FRIEND

When all the world is sleeping,
in my darkest hour.
When I awaken, weeping,
I feel the presence of His power.

When no one seems forgiving
and weary is my soul.
When life seems not worth living,
He helps me reach my goal.

When no one else will listen
to the troubles of my heart,
and on my cheeks tears glisten,
His love He doth impart.

He guides me with a gentle hand
from darkness into light,
until on firm ground I stand,
giving me strength to fight.

To fight the foes within my mind.
To clear away the pain.
He is so gentle and so kind.
He makes me whole again.

I know He will always be there
reaching out to me,
enfolding me in His loving care,
setting my spirit free.

When all others forsake me,
He will be there to the end,
constant and true He will always be,
My Lord, my friend.

Josie Rawson

THE 'LITTLE LADY' WHO CARES!

Take care, Little Lady, as the pages of your life unfold;
There are some of us who love you as your span in time evolves.
You are a gem so precious, a rare stone with brilliant hue,
In a setting that is priceless as befits someone like you.

Your attentive care, your thoughts, concern, for those who are infirm,
The help you give helps us to live; from you much can we learn.
In this verse of pure intent, so meaningful and true
My thoughts add up to one thing - a special thanks from me to you.

No words can explain contentment and sometimes I can feel.
Now my life I find is richer, I look around and see it's real.
Sweet Little Lady, God bless you for all your caring charm.
My good wishes are always with you; may God protect you
                                                    from any harm.

Having you as my friend leaves me no longer alone;
Little Lady, you help enhance my life and bring joy into my home.
To an angel whom I respect, I ply my thanks and gratitude sincere.
May the Lord give me time to continue as we see out each year.

The Little Lady, a *femme fatale*, deceptive beauty so supreme;
Wake me slowly, please take care, don't break my lovely dream.
Forgive my thinking, my intentions, I assure you are honest and true -
To a person so special in my book . . . have you guessed?
                                                    You're right - it's you!

I ask for nothing, and that is what I normally would expect,
But now, with your friendship, in part of my life you are both
                                                    cause and effect.
God bless you, Little Lady, may you have all that you need to survive,
Keep all those whom you care for warm and safe, secure and alive!

But most of all, Little Lady, when thinking of other people's health,
Promise me, you QC/chocolate queen, you will give priority to yourself.
If your love, care, honesty, hard work and sincerity were ever put
to the test,
You would win 'hands down', Little Lady, just because Pat,
you're simply . . . 'the best'!

Tony W Rylatt

SHOCK

They said you were dead,
But that just can't be.
I saw you last week,
Popped round, cup of tea.

They said you were dead,
But what do they know?
Next week we're both going
To see that new show.

They said you were dead,
But I don't understand.
You're always the one
To hold my sad hand.

They shouted you were dead,
But how can that be?
It's always been us two,
Now, is it just me?

Susan Lorkins

A LONG TIME AGO

A long time ago, such a long time ago
How many years? I'm damned if I know

Crow's feet, worry lines, grey hairs galore
She's had two children - I've even more!
Thousands of miles have kept us apart
Though letters, now e-mails tell what's in our hearts

We met in a park, a pre-destined time
Both very nervous we'd not recognise
The other, because we'd inevitably changed
Both late, we pretty much met at the gate

A smile, a 'Hello' and then it was fine
A long time ago, such a very long time

We sat in the sun and drank lots of wine
Hours flew past like the years of our prime
Old friends, old enemies - all had their turn
Photos and memories, eager to learn

Decades of experience, in just one day
Strange how the time just melted away
Too soon it was over, back to our lives
But the joy of our meeting for long will survive

A long time ago, such a long time ago
We smiled, said, 'Goodbye,' then we had to go.

Anne Polhill Walton

FIRM FRIENDS

As infants we were tolerated as each cried for our mums
There was a hint of jealousy but of this we did not succumb
We were too young to know the meaning as we were clothed and fed
Washed and powdered when nature called, then cradled in our beds
As children often suspicious of each other's moods
Although we got on famously, often so much was misconstrued
We had fun together as we sailed this childish life
Becoming firm friends like blood-brothers, counteracting strife

Like twins none suspected as we enjoyed this thrall
Of each other's company and pray God we always will
We satisfied the authorities as we passed our exams
Together taking a challenge as this adult life demands
Degrees and honours did not affect our friendship as it massed
We studied hard and poured our worth, nothing ever marred
Then one day we were called to serve our country very dear
That is when we separated, did anyone see those tears?

You abroad were sent, I could not follow
Being posted to Europe, this war I could not swallow
You were maimed and lost a limb, shell-shocked but alive
Oh how I wished I could have been there to comfort,
                                        thank God you survived
Now an invalid and all that greatness gone
War takes its toll as I too suffered, but not for very long
Sent home to these shores to die, I continually call your name
We two meet and have been made whole again, beyond this veil
                                        there is no shame
Having a lot to catch up on, we renew our friendship vows
Here there is time for everything, as this great one endows
Seeing more clearly and impressed the tenderness that empowers
War is an ugly mess, life should be sweet, all this should be allowed.

R D Hiscoke

I, THE BEHOLDER

Her looks don't draw a second glance
From people who pass by on chance
Her dress is plain without a sheen
She won't attract when she is seen
Within a crowd she blends in well
Just one of many in the swell
But to me, she is my life
This beauty whom I call my wife
Her radiant face displays such love
As any angel up above
Her voice is like a soft refrain
Her soul is pure without a stain
So gentle, kind in all her ways
I'll stay by her for all my days
For I could never ever find
Another woman of her kind
Who gives me all I need in life
This beauty whom I call my wife.

Terence Stephen McNeela

SHARING

The owl and the pussycat were friends, so they say
But where were they going say I?
The object of friendship can not be to drift
With a mere £5 note to get by.

But, there again, if you had nothing to share
And your best friend had plenty to give
You could bet that his money - and sometimes his honey
Would enable you both so to live.

H Hyde

GOODBYE, BARRIE

(A farewell message from your best friend)

Today we celebrate a special life,
For such was Barrie Miller's gift to us
For whom he served, though conscious of the strife
Of failing health, he faced with little fuss.
Our Barrie got great joy from *giving* joy,
By helping, healing, entertaining, by
Participating, adding to the ploy
Of everything around him, never shy!
Psychiatrist at Chorley for the kids,
Club doctor for three clubs at Ramsbottom
And Salford, Stretford too, for bigger kids!
Plus actor, author, poet, with aplomb!
He had so much to give, but now he's gone
And we, still here, give thanks for all he's done.

Christopher Head

SOME OTHER DAY PETER

If people don't die
they would all be stacked
right up to the moon.

I hope it's not my
grandpa has to die,
it is much too soon.

We play together
after school and try
to burst my balloon.

I pretend to cry;
but I really will
should he ever die.

Peter Huggins

GIVING THANKS

He never once didn't understand me; he never once mistook what I said
His voice, like thunder rolling
- An orca calling from the north-west coast
- A cedar tree swaying in the rustling wind
Soft, so delicate as he chanted The Full Moon Song
His voice perfectly tuned to nature, he sang to his mother
Earth - their laughter lifted me.
Wise words woven thro' his stories
Visions woven into his dreams
Freedom and friendship. Justice
Drummed gently into so many lives
And then he had to leave, Beaver Chief. Fred
Healer's heart slipped then into sleep
Keep safe the stories woven in his hair
May feathers softly cradle dreamer's head
'Haitchka'. Your laughter lifted me
We had a similar sense of things
Medicine man from ancient native tribe
Scots girl with a secret Celtic heart
The drum lies silent
The rhythmic music beats within my soul.

Marilyn Hodgson

TO MY DAD

You became a dad to love
Nature decided to give you a call
And you're a father for all
You loved me as a baby and as a child
You stand firm in your ways
Even though I drive you wild
Thanks a million Father for what you've done and do
There's no other father on earth quite like you!

P Edwards

WALKER, WILCOX
(For Sacha)

Classroom meeting,
alphabetical seating,
Walker, Wilcox -
the story kicks off.

Friends together,
finding treasure
in the secrets
kept between us.

Teenage years,
laughs and tears,
drinks in pubs
and nights in clubs.

Then the time
when lads were prime;
names remembered
but best unmentioned!

The years have passed,
gone so fast,
lots of changes -
men and babies.

I must just add,
we would be mad
if we lost touch -
we share too much.

Andrea Sandford

ALONE

You can hear the silence
When you're alone,
When you're on your own
With no one to talk to -

So important to have a friend to talk with
A friend to walk with
To share things, to give -
A friend to have fun with
And good times with -
A friend.

A Hankey

WHAT IS A FRIEND
(For Andrew)

A friend is a paperweight
Holding everything down
A friend is a laugh-a-minute
Custard pie clown

A friend is a shelter
At a rainy, dripping bus stop
A friend is a car ride
On a cold day
A short hop

A friend is a map
When lost at night
A torch
A lamp
A lantern
A map-reading light

A friend is pickle in a sandwich
Chocolate sauce on ice cream
A nice dream
A winning team

Helen Harwood

FRIENDSHIP

Friendship is worth more than one's weight in gold
Friendship is a treasure never to be sold
Friendship is showing how much you really care
Friendship is letting someone know you will be there
Friendship is listening, giving encouragement too
Laughing, crying together, talking it through
Friendship is giving help through good times and bad
A loving touch, a happy smile, to stop you feeling sad
Friendship is a neighbour who's watching out for you
Friendship is special, loyal and true
Friendship is important, through life it plays a part
Friendship fills one's soul with gladness
Friendship comes from the heart.

Linda Mary Hodgson

JONATHAN

I thought we'd never be friends - me and you
People said it couldn't happen,
I listened to them, I believed them
But you made me realise they were wrong.
You made me feel good about myself
You told me I was a good person,
You gave me back my confidence
And helped me find the will to live.
You treated me like a human being
You didn't laugh or judge me,
You accepted me when no one else would
And you let me be myself.
I came so close to giving in,
But you were the one who kept me going,
You gave me strength to fight
And to hold my head up high.
Other people put me down
They hurt me, they made me cry,
Yet even when you weren't around
You dried my tears.
You showed me the light at the end of the tunnel
You showed me life is worth living,
You were so much more than a friend
Because you showed me that love is for giving.

Margaret Ann Scott

To An Old Friend

We walked together up hill and down hill
In a fog so deep the world seemed without substance
We floated non-existent beyond time, beyond feeling
Our conversation meandered until suddenly, unexpectedly
You spoke of a lonely child in a runaway pram
Then you froze to a halt - eyes staring straight ahead
Dead to the present, filled with dreadful presentiment
I held out my hand as if to stop you - only years too late
You roll headlong away from me - the abandoned innocent
It's the shared terrors tangling the threads of our existence that bind us
I am your friend because I have huddled together with you in the dark

In a happier mode we wandered on a warm clear night
You told me a fairytale as if it were all truth
About a land beyond fear ruled by a kind, wise wizard who used
                                        his might to do right
You needed magic shoes to get there - lo, a good witch provided
So clickety clack of your heels, off you went
You soared, and I soared with you on the wings of your conviction

Once when you were small I saw you
But you didn't see me
You were wailing like a trapped animal
Nothing more than a baseball game
But everything to you
You had struck a wall and kept ramming against it to no avail
My soul reached out to you
Years have passed, still stubbornly rearing up walls
Before each impenetrable brick face my heart had shed silent,
                                        angry tears
And I have remembered you as you were then -
A child with a bold chisel-carved face, black eyes blazing in fury
I hope your dreams do not shatter as you scream inwardly
Friend, I wish happiness in starbursts when I wish upon the
                                        night sky for you

Monica Gurney

THANK YOU DEAR MOTHER

Thank you my dear mother
For all of the things that you did
You were always there for me dear
When I was just a kid
You always kissed me better
When I was in pain
The cuddles that you gave me
Soon made me well again
You taught me to do right not wrong
To sing my nursery rhymes to song
Taught me how to tie a lace
How to wash my hands and face
The stories that you conjured up
Were really very grand
About the queen of fairies who lived in fairy land
We always used to laugh a lot
We rarely ever cried
I set a fine example when other children lied
How many millions did I love you
You would ask me every day
Forever and forever more were the words I used to say
A special sort of relationship
Was the one that we both shared
I wish I only had you here to show you how I cared
I did not have you all that long
Only a mere fifteen years
When you had your accident my life was shattered with tears
I know you are an angel now up in heaven above
For every day I think of you as the perfect mother love
Thank you for being my mum, there is nobody around here like you
And I miss you so my dearest mum as only a daughter can do.

Eleanor Brandes-Dunn

MY FRIEND MO

When I was in my teens I met a girl called Mo
We started to get friendly and to the pictures we would go.
We shared each other's confidences and vetted each other's guys
And when we needed an alibi for each other we told lies.

As we grew into adulthood, more sensible we became
We each got married then we realised that life wasn't just a game.
When we had our children we often helped each other too
For life can be quite hectic when you have so much to do.

Now that our families are all grown up and living far away
We meet a lot and always chatter on the telephone each day.
About events and antics of all the folk we know
We share our problems and we laugh about what we did long ago.

But then there is a serious side about our friendship too
In a crisis we can help each other decide what we must do.
I can always rely on her to be right there for me
To listen and to give me loads of tea and sympathy.

My friend Mo . . . or Maureen . . . as I now call her today
Is still my confidante or modern-day counsellor in a way.
I pay tribute to my friend whom I have known for fifty years
For listening to my worries and dispelling all my fears.

Mary Anne Scott

THE VALUE OF A TRUE FRIEND

I called with a friend called Fiona the other day
And I was wondering what on earth she would say
Would she welcome me in at no extra cost
Or would she tell me to go home or get lost?
I know in her life she has helped many
And for this she did not charge them a penny
So I believe for me that she would open her door
And sit down and talk even if she had been doing a chore

Fiona is understanding and patient with others
In the same way that children have trust in their mothers
Sometimes she talks about being a second mother to one
Talking about this always creates a bit of fun
The twelve years of difference is a period quite small
Some might consider it as nothing at all
But to the person concerned it is quite a lot
Second mother you think you are young but you are not!

Fiona has to work hard now each and every day
She cares for her grandchild and loves her in every way
The house she now lives in has still got work to be done
But she knows that she can manage and still have time for fun
The important part of a house is not the carpet or the chairs
But it is knowing that whoever lives in the house really cares
The fact that you care could always be said about you
So may God bless you all the time at everything you do

Robert Doherty

FOR YOU

If I could be
    Somewhere with you
All alone
    Just we two

What would we say?
    Things would be bliss
Feelings we would share
    I would not want to miss

We will walk along
    Looking at the sea
Silent, we may dream
    Of things that may be

Whispering to each other
    Again and again
Hand in hand, laughing
    As we walk in the rain

We would be together
    Everything will be fine
A question I would ask
    Will you ever be mine?

Yes, if I were
    Somewhere with you
Would you ask me
    The same question too?

Joanne H Hale

IN NEED

Words can be spoken, some bonds broken, others forged
a stranger's someone you don't yet know
after a few brief words it's that particular person you will identify with.
Take it upon yourself, your opinions don't count
oh no room for doubt.
From little acorns great oaks grow.
It's the certain person you'll take into your confidence
with a preference you've laid firm foundations
now watch that bond grow into friendship.
It can take a few minutes that can last a lifetime.
Just a knowing glance says it all, that certain person,
they're there through thick and thin with a Cheshire cat grin.
Even in some situations you may not win
it's someone that's there from the start, they share your burdens.
That's when you know your friendships begin
they have become your kith and kin!
That's when a proper friendship can grow, someone you'll always know
come hell or high water through the seasons as they come and go.

Jonathan Covington

WISTFULLY I WONDER

Wistfully I wonder
Where you are tonight
Tears before the thunder
Fall like endless rain
Missing you both day and night
As before, again
Thinking of you constantly
Day and night-time too
Wistfully I wonder
What's become of you

David Bray

ROMANS 8:39
('Nor height nor depth nor any other created thing shall be able to separate us from the love of God which is in Christ Jesus our Lord')

O Father You're my helper
O Father You're my friend
please let Your love embrace me
and uphold me to the end

For whatever may befall me
I know You're always there
to love and to encourage
when no one seems to care

So as I continue on my way
along life's rocky road
the love You give will help me live
in Your will not my own

Ann Langley

A LIFETIME OF LOVE

The roots that you have given to me,
Are foundations created,
For my life to be.
They are precious and treasured,
And live on in my heart,
Though there are many times,
We have been apart.
Don't ever doubt,
How essential you are,
And it matters now,
How near or far.
For across the miles,
You sing to my soul,
Should you forget the words,
I'll make the song whole.

Sue Umanski

THIS LITTLE SILVER RING

The greatest friend I have indeed . . . will never leave my side . . .
Silver is its shine for me . . . as the moon shines on the tide . . .
It has no end or middle . . . but encircles a deepest love . . .
A love that shines with warmth and pride . . . like the sun shines up
above . . .
This thing, I keep, I vow to keep . . . a very precious thing . . .
A token, a band of friendship . . . this little silver ring . . .

Tony Armitage

A LIGHT IN MY LIFE

How quickly our friendship developed.
How easily my love you won
when your eyes my heart enveloped.
What will I do when you're gone?

You've taken me everywhere.
You've been very much my whole world.
With you they can all stand and stare,
for you're my very special little girl.

I smile at the jingle of your harness
as we work and play together.
With you there can be no darkness.
With you, all hardships I'll weather.

Yet I feel how your pace has slowed,
as how differently we measure the years.
Very soon your head will be bowed
and I'll know once again the old fears.

But I'll not forget you, my Connie.
So trusting and loving and wise.
Even if another comes to aid me,
I thank you for being my eyes.

Lynda Bullock

MY CONSTANT FRIEND

I have a friend named Jesus who guards, guides and comforts too,
If He was not constantly by my side, I don't know what I would do,
He sees me through my problems, He guides me when I go wrong,
Although I never realised it, He's been there all my life long,
He comforts me when I'm lonely, He cheers me when I am sad,
When sorrow comes I ask for His help to make things not so bad,
He never lets His friends down, no matter what they do,
You should have Him as your friend and He will be there for you,
Before I met the Lord Jesus, I lived an earthly life,
I always felt no one cared whenever there was any kind of strife,
But since I have Jesus in my life, although I still have cares,
I also have troubles come along, I have problems and have tears,
I just put them before the Lord who helps me see them through,
If you have problems, sorrows or cares that is the thing to do,
Just take the Lord into your life, have Him as your friend,
Then He will take good care of you until life's journey's end,
If we are true and faithful and repay Jesus for His love,
When our earthly life is over we'll be with Him in Heaven above.

Stan Gilbert

WHAT FRIENDS ARE

I was new, and in the neighbourhood too
Having moved house, a traumatic time
No less, if you get my meaning
The house was larger, that meant more cleaning
There was a garden too, for my children, what a gleaning!
A place to play, to feel the air, to sit in the sun,
To have some fun, well, they had somewhere
But I knew no one, and so busy was I then
Three little children, the eldest handicapped,
My work cut out for me, but then, amen
I found myself next door, to an older mother,
Her children still at school, that bit older,
Nice children too, nice father and mother,
And what a friend she proved to be,
Without even my asking too, believe me
To take my son out, and in his wheelchair,
To help with the shopping, plus the washing,
And even, yes! The ironing, I do declare
Making life that wee bit easier,
She proved a real friend, yes! She truly did care
Still today, I thank God for her, and the time we did share together,
As I am a grandmother now you see.

M Lightbody

MEETINGS ON SUNDAYS AT SALVATION ARMY HALL

I go to our meetings on Sunday
The friends I meet there are lovely
There is our captain
Miriam, Doris and Stewart
Peggy, Leonard, Ann and Sue
Bronwen, Megan and Mavis too
Mrs Thomas, Eira, Mr and Mrs Payne and me
Sometimes there are others, maybe two or three
We come together and to Jesus we sing
We speak to Him about everything
We sing our songs to Him with pleasure
Say our prayers all together
Sometimes there are strangers who we make welcome
To share with us in our little temple
So in this house where love never ends
I am glad to pray with all of my friends
Before I finish I would like to say
Thank you dear Lord for every Sunday.

M E Smith

WOMAN FRIEND
(Dedicated to Nicole Lipton)

An ode comes to my heart
Knowing that you are coming back
I've again felt lost and lonely
Since you have been afar

I've been counting the seconds . . .
Hours, days and nights
To greet you back in my life
. . . Friends like you
There aren't two alike

Your loyalty and loving care
I zealously and safely keep
. . . Your healer precious self
Is my fountain . . . my spring

I have missed you daring girl
More than you could realise
. . . You are an essential part
To the harmony in my exile!

You've been my princess . . .
Friend and confidant
And I gratefully thank *God*
For the gift of You, in my life

Describing you in a simple word
You are an honour to human kind
Taming imperfections and fears
. . . My greatest quest of this life

Welcome back dearest Nicole
Welcome back woman friend
. . . One and a thousand times!
Again and again . . . welcome back!

Eduardo Del-Rio Escalona

DEAR FRIEND

She is known as one of life's unfortunate few,
While suffering an illness, which makes her feel blue.
A manic depressive, she bravely carries on,
Struggling until traces of latest low has gone.

Through it all shines her bubbly personality,
Though she's problems of her own, she's been a rock to me.
Always ready to listen, buzzing like a bee,
With a plate of biscuits, cups of hot comforting tea.

S Mullinger

A FRIEND

We waited on the station platform.
The train was delayed.
The friend with me, so nice, but one did not speak to strangers!
Next to us, on a seat, was a hilarious happy family.
Grandma, her daughter, and five boisterous children.
I talked, and joined in their fun.
So exciting, 'Going to London to see the Queen'
I only hoped that they did not expect to see the Queen
Resplendent in robes, and wearing a tiara!
Sometimes to a child, it is a 'let down'.
The train was approaching, and I wished them all a happy day,
And gave the children some pocket money.
The youngest said to Grandma,
'Who is the lady?'
Grandma smiled at me and answered, 'A friend.'
It made my - and my friends', happy day.

Madeline Chase Thomas

JUST LIKE MOTHERS DO

I called my mum today,
I was feeling a little blue.
She soon cheered me up,
Just like mothers do.
She gave me words of encouragement,
Inspiration and love,
Sending our prayers,
To our Lord God above.
I love her so much,
She just has that way,
To pick me up and brush me down,
Getting me through my day.
She has a magic Midas touch,
I want you all to see,
Brushing away my heartfelt tears,
She's so special to me.

Dawna-Mechellé

PIGEON PAIR - MY BEST FRIENDS

Have you ever thought
When the children are small
How the time flashes by
And you've not realised at all?

They grow up so fast
And when it's too late
You look back in sorrow
And then have to wait
To recollect the how and the why and the when
All those dear little ways which they had - now and then!
You can't quite remember, can't just recall
And now look at them both, they're so big and so tall

Your mind flashes back to the moment of birth
The joy and the happiness, laughter and mirth
But - just wait a minute, wait there and pause -
Those very wee bundles are yours, all yours
To cosset and love for the rest of your life
For all of your days, through trouble and strife
'The thought of it terrifies, petrifies me,
I'll just never cope - but I will, just you see'
You did too and watched all the ups and the downs
The laughter and tears, the smiles and the frowns
The look in the eyes when Mummy was there
And Daddy was too, to love and to care
To teach all the rules about football and cricket
And tell them the difference 'tween the pitch and the wicket

Mum played with their dolls and taught them to sew
To knit and to cook hoping they'd get to know
How everything worked in a family frame
But none was too serious, all mostly a game

The time has just flown but your memories are there
Of your two lovely children, a real pigeon pair
Lots of love given and then lots returned
And respect on both sides most certainly earned.

They're flying the nest now, they'll be on their own
With those seeds of knowledge Dad and Mum have both sown
To give and not take, to know right from wrong -
Live life to the full and I pray it be long

Paddy Jupp

SUMMER MEMORY

Air humid, sky changing from grey to pastel blue
Clouds skim by
Dog Rene tongue gently touching
My fingers perspiring
I was oblivious to a time he wouldn't be with us
As I soaked up the sun, brow tilted upwards
He watched as I settled on a rock
Did he know he hadn't long
When he stopped to gaze so lovingly
Before stepping over some dried up mud?
Happy memories of the friend we always remember
Giving always his love.

Ann Parr

DEDICATION TO A CLOSE FRIEND

How can one so define a friend?
P'haps someone on whom you depend
When life's begun to feel unfair,
To lend an ear, to sweeten care,
To put you back on an even keel,
Because you know they really *feel*
And care for how life's treating you
By offering help, and thoughts anew.

A true friend's like a healing gift
That always gives the soul a lift.
We're sometimes seen at our best,
At other times perhaps depressed,
But the bond is there, whate'er we do,
We cannot break a friendship true.
It helps to make our life worthwhile,
Helps us face it with a smile.

So let us give our thanks above
For the gift of friendship and of love,
Dedicating this to our very close friend,
Who colours our life, our thanks we send.

Lola Perks-Hartnell

SHE IS

She is a pear, tough on the outside and soft and juicy in the inside.
She is a tiger, she can be fierce and she can be soft and loveable.
She is as sleek and quiet as a flute playing softly.
She is a wizard, wise and wonderful and full of ideas.
She is yellow, as yellow as the burning sun on a summer's day.
She is a computer, ready to give off great advice.
She is the water that trickles down my veins.
She is a diamond, looking in the water at its glass-like figure.
She is a slug, sucking up my thoughts.
She is an armchair that I curl up in which keeps me comfy.
She is the snow that falls upon me when I play in the garden.
She is my teddy that I go up to when I am sad.

Amy Leeder (9)

THE HAPPY TRIO

Baby, mother, grandmamma,
The trio is complete,
Three happy people, life for them
Is good and very sweet.

For Grandma finds fulfilment,
In her daughter's perfect joy,
And mother has her first born son,
A little baby boy.

Oh may the years be very kind,
No tears or fears or frowns,
Yet changes come, babies grow up,
Life is all ups and downs.

But you may cling together,
As you go the winding way,
And be a happy little trio,
As you are today.

D A Sheasby

TRUE FRIENDSHIP

They sat side by side, in the old village school,
Both of them five years of age,
This was their first day of learning,
They were starting on very first page.
Time passed so quickly, they had shared many things,
Troubles and laughter and tears,
Then came the time when their school days were through,
And each had to choose a career.
So now their lives changed for the work that they chose,
Sent them in different ways,
But they never lost touch wherever they went,
For a friendship like theirs wouldn't fade.
Through many years they'd both married,
Had a family, two girls and two boys,
What parties they had when the families met up,
Music and laughter and noise.
It is now seventy years since they'd sat side by side
In their desks at the old village school,
Now on their own, they are arguing still,
But neither gives in as a rule!
As I look at my mum and her friend Aunty May,
I have learnt through the years one special thing,
Not many today can have seen in their life
What a pleasure a real friend can bring.

Dinah Court

SO MUCH MORE THAN A FRIEND

Dear Thomas we have had our moments,
Some not so good but we overcame them,
For true friends do have problems
Yet we are better than that. Just an unpleasant interlude.

When I'm feeling down and extremely blue
I pick up the telephone and hear your laughter,
I know it is important to carry my life through,
You are a tonic and an awful lot wiser.

Thank you dear Thomas for being there,
I just wish I could do so much more,
However, my life has been enhanced with your care,
I am lucky to have a soulmate so dear.

Jay Baker

LOST IN TIME

Lost in time,
Tide and thought,
Confused by mem'ries time has bought.
Pulsed by heartache,
Laced with pain,
Can the clock of time turn for us again?
Good times, mostly the ones we remember,
The bad,
And sad,
Now far lost and gone forever.
Your looks have stayed, tho' you have changed,
Whilst my love for you is forever framed,
Where we cannot go forward for looking back,
To erase the feeling that burns our hearts.

J S Liberkowski

MY GOOD FRIEND

Many friends have rallied round
Helping me keep my feet on the ground
Getting me through a recent loss
No matter what it has cost

My neighbour has helped in every way
Keeping my spirits up each day
Nothing has been too much for her
No, she could not have done any more

We have not been lifetime friends
But I will thank her to the end
She is like a sister to me now
I hope she never moves away

So with thanks to a neighbour so very kind
Before she arrives to change my mind
I will send this poem to you
If it's the last thing I do.

Jean Bradbury

JACQUI

I'm sitting on a red bus which slowly wends its way
To the fine city of Norwich where I'm off to spend a day
When we reach our destination and the final stopping place
I will scan the people round me for that dear familiar face
When a tall, slim, dark-haired girl I see
My heart with pride will swell
For this one person means to me far more than words can tell
What, you may ask, is so special about this girl so fair?
She is to me a daughter and one beyond compare.

Barbara King

DEAREST FRIEND
(To H from B)

When in my mind I balance all my woes
against the joy that from your brightness springs,
and weigh the heavy weight that with them goes
against the lightness your dear presence brings;
and when in your expressive eyes a tear,
softening laughter, takes compassion's part,
and in the mischief of your voice I hear
the gentle music of your playful heart -
Oh then (strange alchemy!) your lightness turns
the scale of worldly values upside down;
all debts diminish and dull care adjourns
when subject to the sway of your bright crown:
If wealth be marked by weight when it is told,
your lightest glance of love were heaviest gold.

Bernard Brown

OUR PAL

That small soft bundle we first carried home
has stayed a faithful friend through all the years.
Enjoyed our romps and play when out to roam
and gave us pleasure - chased away our tears.

The fussing of the children when they saw
that tiny tail, pink tongue and whiskery snout.
They loved him when we first came through the door
what fun there was when we all romped about.

The first to wake on mornings and to greet
by dashing up the stairs so craftily.
And then the bedclothes pulled from off our feet
and children chased from bedrooms hastily.

His favourite blanket, slipper and his bone
to hide them all we tried but soon he found.
The game he loved to play when on the phone
we had no peace when friends they came around.

If strangers came he soon would let us know
his bark was different and we soon were taught.
By wagging tail or ruffled hairs would show
and so excited when his lead was brought.

We knew like us that he was growing old
now greying whiskers and his slowing trot.
But all that time he trusted us to be
his lifetime pal - he will not be forgot.

Alan J Vincent

FAMILY AND FRIENDS

Why do we hate
the people
who protect us?
We never understand
anything they do or say.
We never listen
anyway.
They are older,
they know more.
When we grow up
we'll know the score.
They are wiser,
their knowledge deep.
There's
nothing they can do,
to keep from feeling
sad
when our lives
fall apart
and everything looks bad.
They comfort us
and help us through.
We should be saying - 'We love you!'

Maxene Huntley

SOMETIMES

Comfort, joy, hope, love and happiness,
A stark contrast to my naked loneliness.
As I reach out and you're not there,
Sometimes I think you do not care.

Concern, worry, dread, hate and sadness,
A parallel for my unforgiven badness.
As I reach out and you're not there,
Sometimes I think you do not care.

I close my eyes to seek relief,
I only sneeze out tears of grief.
As I reach out and you're not there,
Sometimes I think you do not care.

Hugh S McKay

ONE AND ONLY!

When you find your one and only love,
Your world starts spinning in the clouds above,
The one thing on your mind is so strong,
Even though you think it may be wrong,
Whenever you talk, everything is fine,
You talk to let them know they're constantly on your mind,
Your whole body is tranquil, your mind is set free,
Into your own dreams and faze of mystery,
The smiles and the tears will come and go,
But at the end of each day, your strong love will always show,
The fear of you losing the dream, makes you sick,
But you hope and pray it will be there through thin and thick,
All you can say is you love the only thing that is right,
The one thing that keeps you safe at night,
I love you, need you, dream and care for you,
In everything I do I want to share with you.

Sade Davies

PHILOSOPHY

Love is the oxygen to our soul,
Without it there is just empty space,
It breathes light and fuels our bodies,
Love is the answer to our life.

Death is the pathway to a new beginning,
A greater world and a more powerful life,
In order to have life we must inevitably,
Have death to even out the odds.

Life is the greatest gift,
It opens up the realm of possibilities,
And allows you to be free,
It is the form of our existence.

Kimberly Harries

ONE WISH

If only I could have one wish
I know what it would be
I would give up all that I have
To have a day that's depression free.

A big dark cloud surrounds me
Tears flow freely every day
Sleep doesn't end the torture
It just leads to another day.

I beg for someone to cling to
To tell me it will be okay
As I pace around in agony
I keep praying it will go away.

I can't explain to everybody
I know what some will say
'Pull yourself together'
They turn and walk away.

I do not want your pity
Or your sympathy
Just wish me a day tomorrow
That is full of peace and tranquillity.

Pauline Drew

I WISH I WAS HERE

No telephone rings to press against my ear,
But that does not matter because I'm not really here.
No visitor knocks my door to bring good cheer,
But that does not matter because I'm not really here.
No letter is sent with news decisive and clear,
But that does not matter because I'm not really here.
No grandchildren visit except in prayer,
But that does not matter because I'm not really here.
Nightmares night after night, I tremble with fear,
But that does not matter because I'm not really here.

Jay Baker

ONE WISH

To have a single wish
how often has one thought
if this miracle could come true
the choice of what to wish for
is left alone for you.

One wish, what can it be?
You must not waste the chance
think carefully and well
all you could ever want
yours and yours alone to tell.

Peace on earth for all
that is such a noble thought
no strife, no wars, no misery
if one wish could make it happen
what a better world it would be.

One wish is all I have
so what is it to be?
I racked my brains all night
and all that I can wish for
Lord! Please put the world to rights.

Geoff Hume

WHO REMEMBERS DIANA?

Who remembers Diana
Who remembers the day,
When in a Paris underpass
She was cruelly snatched away?

Diana was swept to glory
A girl of just nineteen,
So innocent and trusting
But fate would intervene.

I wish I could have known her
Beauty personified!
The darling of a nation
A radiant young bride.

Unequal to the pressure
And grievously betrayed,
Thus sadly disillusioned
From her own path she strayed.

She couldn't face rejection
And so she looked for love,
That was her true quest in life
Everything else above.

A Queen she never would have been
But was the Queen of Hearts,
And in her short, sad lifetime
She played so many parts.

How rarely she is mentioned
How easy to forget,
But as five years approaches
I will remember yet.

Diana held hands with lepers
And could communicate,
With people from all walks of life
From humble to the great.

The scope of her potential
We now will never know,
Her tragic and untimely end
A cataclysmic blow.

Moira Wiggins

THE PRETTY PLANET

Seeing the Earth through the windows of the space capsule,
We could see the beautiful blues and greens below;
It all looked so wonderful,
But it showed how minute we are in every way.
Just plodding our way through life,
Our allotted span is so very short.

So little time to live.
So little time to love and be loved,
Trying to achieve great things -
Some of us will do just that.

Medicine had eradicated some diseases,
Mankind is living far longer.

If only we could all live in some sort of limbo,
Where the Devil and evil thoughts are banished forever,
But this I am sorry to say is only just a dream!

Valerie Willan

ONE WISH FOR ME

My one wish would be
To see my parents who gave birth to me
Let them return from the dead
As young as the day they were wed
Not in pain as they went
With the reaper's agents disease and spent

In retrospect it would confuse them both
To see their daughter yet to be born
With her face full of wrinkles, looking sad and forlorn
Still grieving for her dear mum and dad
And whose selfish attitude is really too bad

So my one wish would be
To rid this world of the big, big 'C'

Susan Lewis

SOMETIMES I WISH

Sometimes I wish I knew you better,
That I could see things as you do,
I, who am always with you,
Seem so far away.
I wonder how life will treat you,
If you will love and be loved,
I welcome each day I am with you,
And fear each day we are apart.

Sometimes I wish I was better,
At giving you all you need,
At letting you go,
And trusting you will return to me.
I wonder if you are content,
Can you see my love?
Do I show you when I smile when I cry?
I fear all I do is wrong.

Sometimes I wish I knew you better,
With time, maybe I will learn,
You seem so small,
In my arms safe, so quiet.
I wonder where we will be, you and I,
In ten, twenty, thirty years' time.
Will we be together and happy?
That is all I can wish for.

Caroline Ayre

GRANT ME THIS WISH

Come down from Heaven, a wish come true
For you to grant me a life with you
My body it crumbles with illness that's rife
And am I so humble with you in my life?

Many wishes I've made for my body renew
Life never fades, made from honey and dew
Deep in my heart I know you do dwell
Bringing me peace and making me well

And standing by me I'm never alone
Contentment I seek from the Heavenly throne
Grant me this wish for my body renew
My hands are a dish for your Heavenly fruit

Fill me with love and comfort me still
Come down from above to give me the will
Give me the strength to continue my life
Grant me your wealth through illness that's rife

Ester Francisca Caruana

A THOUGHT FOR OUR TIME

If I ruled the world
I could be whatever I want to be,
Everything, would be possible for me,
I could be a singer of beautiful songs,
I could be a righter of everyone's wrongs,
The creator of all things good,
But that doesn't mean that I would!
To find one's self in this position
What a dreadful, frightening mission,
The ultimate power of life and death,
The ability to control all pain and suffering,
To be responsible for joy and laughter,
To control the present and the hereafter,
The more I think of it, the more it gets dafter,
But ridiculous as this might be
It's worth a thought or three,
For there are people in this world
Whose ambition is to control you and me,
And you and I must make it clear,
That we will not be fooled, nor be ruled by fear!

Bah Kaffir

I WISH

I wish someone
Would love me,
And think the whole world
Of me.
Hold on to my hand
When we walk,
Look into my eyes
When we talk.
Give me a hug
When they are near,
Or a smile, or a kiss
Say they're pleased
To see me here
And hope I always will be.

Karen Cook

PIPE DREAMS

I wish for:-
> Changes in so many ways. Am I alone
> In wanting truth instead of spin?
> A politician I can put my trust in.

I wish for:-
> A fair Referendum, that the 'antis' win.
> Greater strength for democracy,
> With limits on the growth of beaurocracy.

I wish for:-
> 'No' to autocracy and neocracy.
> Help for those seen as second-best,
> Without the indignity of a means test.

I wish for:-
> Peace in Northern Ireland, a country at rest,
> But not by way of compromise.
> Surrender to violence can not be wise.

I wish for:-
> Proof that ever greater European ties
> Will merely make us pay the price
> Of loss of fiscal independence, not nice.

I wish for:-
> Free speech, a British Britain; let it suffice
> To say I've wishes, many more,
> Am I old fashioned? Anyway, I wish for . . .

Stephen Ramsden

SOLITUDE

Hedgerows bereft of creatures of the earth,
Aloft, no wings alive across the skies,
In fields no cattle, no gregarious rabbit or reclusive fox
Disturbs the mantle of the covering green,

Today the world is mine,
On lease for these few fleeting moments,
A covetous possession and for this duration - mine.

Time for a mind to clear itself of care,
Time to absorb and be absorbed by peace,
Time for a heart to beat afresh and love,
Time to admit a reawakening of the soul.

To be alone, not lonely, just alone,
Unique in solitude and sweet tranquillity,
In solitary state for this brief instant,
Is where I am and where I wish to be.

Barry Jones

THE DANCE

As I was walking home one night
my eyes beheld an eerie sight.
A dark man standing straight and tall
beside the graveyard's stony wall.

'Come - dance with me,' I heard him say,
his voice familiar, but far away.
I knew this man! How could this be?
Tears filled my eyes. I could not see.

The years together had gone so fast.
Twelve months ago my dear one past.
Away to where I could not follow.
My days and nights now cold and hollow.

From echoes lost his sweet voice came,
like angels singing, he called my name.
'Let's play beneath the velvet night.
The moon is full, the stars are bright.'

As in a trance, my mind in shock,
he led me down the churchyard walk.
I heard the sound of music playing.
'Don't let me wake,' my heart was praying.

I felt his hand slip into mine.
We swayed, as one, through endless time.
Locked in his arms - a sweet embrace,
I saw once more my loved one's face.

In the gentle dawning's light
As he began to fade from sight,
I heard him whisper in my ear,
'I will return - I'll meet you here.

We'll dance until the day you're laid
beside me in my lonely grave.
Goodbye my love. Don't shed a tear.
Just call my name - I'm always near.'

Polly Davies

THE GYPSY

A gypsy I would like to be
And travel round the country.
I would have a caravan for all to see,
I would call it my Rosealee.

I would call at the farm for my eggs,
And have a chat about the weather.
If I am lucky I will sell some pegs,
And give them some lucky heather.

I would have two dogs called Meg and Marc,
Be up in the morning with the lark,
I would look for work picking plums,
Work very hard till night-time comes.

When day is over I would meet with friends,
We would all sit round the camp fire,
Talking about the day as it ends,
That would be my life's desire.

May Ward

WISHING OR WASTING

I think that a wish is an agnostic prayer,
Making a request to someone, but you don't know who's there.

Have we the ability to know what to ask for?
Do you know what is best for you, are you really sure?

Perhaps you need guidance, to know what is best,
Do you really want to put yourself to the test?

So let's not get bogged down, asking for wealth,
Just stick to the obvious, constant good health.

Trevor Napper

WISHING

Sometimes you have a wish,
a wish you cannot share,
a wish so special and personal,
no one would listen or care.

To you that wish is everything,
something you dream about,
you know one day you'll get it,
then you'll scream and shout.

They think I'll never make it,
they tell me all the time,
they think if I don't tell them,
I'll never make it mine.

But I know life is different,
That my dreams will come to me,
That if I wait and persevere,
Dreams can be reality.

Allison Bridge

PRESENTS

What shall I buy your for Christmas?
What can I get just for you?
Should I buy chocolates or flowers?
I just don't know what to do.

How would you fancy some music,
Cassettes by a group in England?
Or aren't you allowed to play music like that?
Perhaps it's already been banned.

Might a new toy be in order,
Something to warm up your bed?
Everyone here has a teddy, you know,
And all you can see is its head!

I've heard that if you believe in
Fairy tales they will come true.
I'd like to try it, and maybe
You will believe in them too.

Both people must make the same wish
If you're to have it come true.
Trouble is, can I be certain
I made the same wish as you?

Look in my heart and you'll soon find
Just what I wanted to see.
Christmas at home by the fireside,
You with your family (and me!).

Presents will not last forever
Christmases come and they go
But, one thing I'll always treasure -
My love for you. Make it grow.

Peter Meredith

MY WISH

If my wish was granted
I would be judge and jury
for the day.
I'd lock away
the paedophiles
and throw away the keys,
and after that
I'd round up all the terrorists
and their ammunition too,
then drown them in the sea.
I'd make the unemployed
tidy up the streets
then I'd ban all drunk drivers
never to drive again.
I could go on forever,
but I won't
because I know
wishes don't come true.

E Bevans

I Wish

I wish my wish would come true
That this whole world would be renewed
No more evil deeds being done
That peace will come to everyone
Prayers being answered, churches filled
Everywhere throughout this world

I wish, I wish and wish again
That man would brother be with man
Try and help - and do not hinder
Be useful, hopeful and be kinder
Though your words to them may seem
Impossible to believe - and just a dream

Jean Logan

IF I COULD...

If I could work a miracle
I know what it would be
I'd just turn back the hands of time
and keep you here with me

If I could work a miracle
then you would have no pain
I'd wipe away the endless hurt
and make you well again

If I could work a miracle
this nightmare would go away
I'd wake up on a sunny morn
and you'd be here to stay

If I could work a miracle
once more our lives we'd fill
with endless dreams and hopes and plans
and we'd be happy still

But I can't work a miracle
so what else can I do?
Just give you one more hug and kiss
and say goodbye to you

Christine Lannen

Only A Dream

If I could have one wish come true,
It's for peace of mind and content,
To be able to pay my dues and demands
And have something left at the end.
To go away on holiday,
Treat my family and friends.
I would also like to stay healthy and fit,
To gain money I wouldn't mind
One little bit.
I would go on a shopping spree,
Take friends and family, and
Save some for a rainy day
To be able to have a wish come true.
I would look after him and her
And never feel blue.

J Nicholls

IF ONLY

If only I could paint or sing
Instead of trying faltering rhyme,
I'd steal from every shining thing
The light that outlasts thieving time;

Find where the sun stores molten gold,
Fold deeply in my brush, and take,
While the bright veiling clouds unfold,
Light from that great unfathomed lake;

And where in night the pale stars hide
Their pools of diamonds, casting gleams
On sea and moors and hills spread wide,
Dip a dark brush in silver streams.

I'd take the colours of the day
And paint my dreams in pictures bright,
Or sing their wonder in a lay
That caught the music of the light.

Then with a flute among the hills
And misty slopes of silver dew
I'd steal the sound of mountain rills
And turn that into music too.

But why, I thought, since words can sing,
Can conjure visions from sunbeams,
Of winter gone, or coming spring,
Or simply rainbows out of dreams:

Pick up a pen and pray for wings
To fly into the source of light,
Drink deep of those mysterious springs
So words may sing, paint pictures bright.

Diana Momber

IF I COULD FLY

If I could fly!
I'd swoop beneath the showery sky
And seek the darling buds of May;
Rest where the wind had bade me stay . . .
If I could fly.

If I could soar!
I'd touch the blue of heaven's door;
Then skim the waves of sparkling seas
Where palm trees whisper on the breeze . . .
If I could soar.

If I could glide!
Upon the wings of morn I'd ride;
I'd never touch the earth beneath
But to the sun my joy bequeath . . .
If I could glide.

Earthbound I stay;
Yet see the birds on branches sway;
I feel their joy upon the wing
Reach out to greet the growing spring . . .
Still, dreams can stay!

Evelyn Balmain

THE RAMBLER'S LAST WISH

To awaken once more
To the chorus at dawn
And remember the days
When leaves start to fall
I'd wander through valleys
All covered in fern
Then listen intently
To hear the birds call
If once more again
I could do all this
Then that my friends
Is my dearest wish

F Dunn

OUR PARADISE

To feel the powerful heat of the sun beating down,
To hear the songbirds with their tuneful melodies,
To smell the freshness of the morning air,
To taste the tropical fruits on each new day,
And to wake with the knowledge that new places can be explored,
is our paradise.

Our paradise is being together and exploring the world on our holidays
Our paradise is being free to roam wherever we please.
Our paradise is being able to look at the world around us and smile,
Knowing we are happy here.

Visiting exotic new places, seeing new scenery,
Swimming deep blue oceans and climbing the tallest mountains.
This is the beauty we know. This is our paradise.

Tracey Burgon

HOLYLAND

Where would I like to be?
Walking the shores of Galilee.
Where fishermen cast their net,
Where Jesus, His disciples met.
Where Jesus calmed the raging sea,
That's where I would like to be.

What would I like to see?
The garden at Gethsame,
Where Jesus knelt in prayer,
His disciples, sleeping there,
Unaware of what was to be.
That's what I would like to see.

What would I like to do?
Visit Jerusalem, Nazareth, Bethlehem, too,
To see where Jesus once lived,
Maybe, climb, the Mount of Olives,
See Calvary, where Jesus died, for me and you.
That's what I would like to do.

Joan Williams

WISHFUL THINKING

It's wishful thinking that drifts me off into a dream,
Taking me back to those wonderful times,
Whenever I hear the sound of romance,
As the radio plays our favourite dance.
As my heart begins to leap,
The thought of you brings a tap to my feet.
For I remember so well holding you tight,
When we danced away into the night.
Now our youth has long since gone,
But still our romance lingers on.

Elisabeth Dill Perrin

LIFE IS PRECIOUS - SO LIVE IT

Shafts of sunlight pierce the sky
As night surrenders to dawn,
Early morning mists drift over the meadows
Poppies waltz to a breeze in the corn.
A sleepy toad on the edge of a brook
Opens and closes one eye,
A glint of green and iridescent blue
As a kingfisher darts close by.
So much to enjoy in God's beautiful world
Don't waste a precious minute,
Grasp each day and hold it fast,
Welcome it, enjoy it and *live* it.

Jean Mackenzie

A SINGLE WISH

One wish is all I need,
A wish combined with hope,
A wish where I succeed,
And one that helps me cope,
One wish is all I pray for,
A wish so dear to me,
A wish I live all day for,
Is that you were here with me.

One wish is all I ask of life,
A wish that life denies,
I've wished that you were in my world,
A world that I despise,
Oh Father, how I wish that you
Were here with me today,
Oh Father how I do miss you,
More than words can say.

A single wish,
Forever so,
A worthless wish?
I'll never know,
But a single wish, with me I'll keep,
I'll continue wishing while I sleep.

Adrian Godfrey

COUNTING ON FINGERS

Counting is fun!
You start at one,
When you say two -
What you can do
Is count to three.
If you want more
Then go to four!
After you say five
You know you'll strive
To get to six
And be the first who picks
Up number seven.
You'll think it's heaven
When you say eight
And you're feeling great!
At number nine
You're feeling fine -
When you reach ten
Your wish will be to start again!

Lynne Done

THE OFFICE

For a moment
I raised my eyes from my work
In this cold, damp gloomy room
From which I can only see
A grey graffitied concrete wall

And I dreamed of being
Where bougainvillaea grows
Where citrus scents the air
And cicadas rasp their rhythms
In the stillness of the early afternoon
I dreamed
I could pluck grapes from the vine
And watch the lengthening rectilinear shadows
Of the spreading palm fronds
As I basked in the tender caress
Of Helios himself

For a moment only
I raised my eyes from my work
As I dreamed

Nicholas Howard

EMPTY HEART

Fill this space
with life's embrace.
Fill this lonely spot
with something hot.
Consume and intrigue
with deep emotions.
Surpass all else
In total - heavenly,
sublime - devotion.

Gary J Finlay

OUR WISH

As a foster carer I see lots of heartache and pain,
I watch these little scraps as confidence they gain.
They come to me a woeful soul, so sad and all alone,
But soon inside my own front door they're made to feel at home.
It might be babies or toddlers sweet or older I never know,
But with lots of love and caring we see our children grow.
One Saturday we watch with ease, the lottery is drawn,
Two of my little darlings, a wish from them is born.
'If you won the lottery,' this wish they said to me,
'Would you adopt the two of us?' a third one said and me.
A lump rose inside my throat, I turned to hide my tear,
I found myself then praying, 'This wish Lord, did you hear?'

Christine Ianson

THE GREATEST CHRISTMAS GIFT

At Christmastime we now commit
Ourselves to follow in God's way,
As God guides us along His path
Giving new blessings every day.
But what is the greatest Gift? I ask -
That all humankind be filled with His love,
I pray.

Michael Thompson

BUTCH'S VOYAGE

August bank holiday Monday,
At around about twenty to three,
Poor Butch's boat ride on the great river Styx
Departed from Southend on sea.

The sun shone as Mum came to guide him,
The sky was a deep shade of blue,
But that was the saddest bank holiday,
I've ever had to get through!

Mick Nash

SUBMISSIONS INVITED
SOMETHING FOR EVERYONE

POETRY NOW 2002 - Any subject,
any style, any time.

WOMENSWORDS 2002 - Strictly women,
have your say the female way!

STRONGWORDS 2002 - Warning!
Age restriction, must be between 16-24,
opinionated and have strong views.
(Not for the faint-hearted)

All poems no longer than 30 lines.
Always welcome! No fee!
Cash Prizes to be won!

Mark your envelope (eg *Poetry Now) 2002*
Send to:
Forward Press Ltd
Remus House, Coltsfoot Drive,
Peterborough, PE2 9JX

**OVER £10,000 POETRY PRIZES
TO BE WON!**

Judging will take place in October 2002